Finding Courage

A True Story of One
Woman's Victory Over
Devastating Trials

Blessings to you!
Helen Mulligan

H. W. P. Mulligan

Printed in Canada

ISBN: 978-1-4866-1952-8
eBook ISBN: 978-1-4866-1953-5

Word Alive Press
119 De Baets Street Winnipeg, MB R2J 3R9
www.wordalivepress.ca

Cataloguing in Publication information can be obtained from Library and Archives Canada.

To our wonderful Creator God. Without Him, I would not be.

Acknowledgments

To all those lovely people who have been there for me and helped me in my journey, thank you! You know who you are. You have been, and are, a wonderful inspiration and encouragement to me. Most of all, a big thank you goes to my husband Ron and my sister-in-law Anne for editing and helping me improve my story.

Introduction

I've lived through a lot of the same things so many others have experienced in their lives. In this book, I focus on our God who gave me the same help that is available to everyone.

When I began writing this story, I thought that I only needed to write in order to work through a memory that surfaced while I was dealing with my first husband's drinking and neglect. But then, because God helped me so much, I realized that these words need to be shared.

In order to make this story easy to relate to, I've left out the religion I was brought up in, the names of everyone involved, and the part of Canada I was born in and where I used to live.

My prayer is that no matter what you are going through, you will be encouraged and helped by my story.

Chapter One

A red swimsuit at a swimming hole should have brought me much enjoyment! I made it myself when I was sixteen years old. It had turned out very nicely. I was proud of it. It's a puzzle to me why I didn't keep it. How come I ended up giving it away?

There are other things that puzzle me. Something is missing from my memory. Why are there so many gaps in what I remember? I think my childhood was good.

I was born in a little log cabin into a conservative and isolated community in the Canadian backwoods in the middle of the twentieth century. I was the fifth child in a very large family. You can imagine the noise in our house!

One Sunday, my older siblings went to visit their friends. Mom and Dad and the little ones were having a nap. While walking into the kitchen with my sister, closest to me in age, I looked at her in amazement. It was so quiet that we could hear the clock ticking! We had not heard that before!

About every year and a half, our mom would bring home a new baby. She loved all her babies, and each one was very special to her. How she was able to do that is beyond me. She said, "With God you can do anything!"

My dad was a teacher in a private school. He had a bad leg from a farming accident that happened when he was young and couldn't work on the farms like most of the men did in our community.

The first home I remember was in one half of a building that was also used as a school classroom during the week and for church services on Sundays. I remember walking into that room when I was five years old and looking at my dad teaching from the pulpit. I was awed by the bigness of the room and by my dad. My oldest sister quickly took me back to the other half of the building to Mom. I was still too young to be in school.

Another memory that has stayed with me is that I got too big to sit on Dad's knee. The younger kids needed his attention, but I remember wanting to be held, too!

My first school experience took place in a different private school. By then, my dad was managing my uncle's store. I remember reciting the times tables with the other children. The girls sat on one side of the classroom and the boys on the other.

When I was nine years old, I got to go to the public school which had just been built in our community. I loved being at school, I thought school was the best thing ever!

After school and on weekends, I played outside most of the time with the neighbourhood kids, my older sister, and my younger brother. We spent lots of time exploring our acreage, building little houses with sticks, and crawling through barbed-wire fences. They weren't easy to crawl through! Wouldn't you know it, one day I ripped my new red denim dress which Mom had just made for me. And that was the first time I had worn it!

In winter, we often went outside in the dark, lying on our backs in the snow looking up at the stars, the moon, and the northern lights. Sometimes at night we would play shadow tag in winter. We would run through the light from the windows, and if the one who was "it" stepped on my shadow, then I was "it!"

One day my parents got a letter from Mom's sister, asking if she could have just one of us kids because she couldn't have any of her own. My mother's answer was, "No, I can't give even one away. Which one could I give up? I love them all too much.

Even though I sometimes felt lost among so many, this was my family and I belonged with them.

On my tenth birthday, we moved south to work on a sugar beet farm. We spent one whole summer hoeing beets.

It was during this time that my mother showed me the power of prayer. My dad and most of the other kids had gone to work on one of the fields far away from our house and I stayed home to help Mom with the little ones. In the afternoon, greyish-green clouds came up. I'd never seen them like that! We had been bathing the little ones in a tub outside because it was so hot, We rushed inside as the rain began to fall—and then the golf-ball-sized hail!

My mother got down on her knees and prayed for safety for Dad and the children with him. On the way home, he had to drive through a deep valley. At the bottom of the valley, the road was built up high to cross a creek. There were no guardrails on either side and he could hardly see in front of him with the rain pouring down so hard, but they made it home safely. That was a wow moment! God had protected them because Mom had prayed!

When I was eleven years old, I had appendicitis and nearly died. My appendix burst during the operation and my insides became badly infected. After three weeks in the hospital, I was well enough to go home. When my sister told me that Dad had called all of my family together to pray for me, I was again awed by the power of prayer.

At the hospital, they woke me up very early in the mornings, and I continued to wake up early once I was back home. These early mornings allowed me to read my New Testament while I waited for Mom and Dad to get up.

Every day I heard birds singing in the bushes near our window. It was so sweet, so pure, so lovely, and so altogether heavenly to hear them singing first thing in the morning. What a beautiful start to each new day!

After having been looked after so well in the hospital, I decided that I wanted to be a nurse, just like the ones who had taken such good care of me. They had all been so kind to me. I thought it would be great if I could be like them and help others in the same way.

My love of reading began while I was in the hospital. Someone there brought me a book to read, and the story was so interesting that it took the pain away. Later I wrote this little essay in school:

I Like Books

I like books. I like the looks of books. I like the feel of books. I like the look of a well-worn Bible. I like the feel of an all new math book like my sister has. I like a little book that I can slip into my pocket. I like to see a shelf full of books. I like to run my fingers over books, they've a good feeling, books have. I like everything about books, but most of all I like to read them!

At the age of thirteen, I asked Jesus to come into my life. Reading the Bible and the many Christian storybooks that our teachers brought into our library helped me to see that I needed Him. My parents were believers in the Bible, and that also helped me.

Many times I prayed the same prayer. I wanted to be sure that Jesus was in my heart. Then I noticed my attitude changing. I enjoyed getting the kindling (woodchips) ready for Dad to start the fire in the kitchen stove on cold winter mornings, and I wanted to help Mom with the babies. Many nights when my little sister cried and cried, I rocked her in the baby carriage so that Mom could get some sleep.

As I grew older and observed the relationships between my parents and many other people, I began to believe that being a girl made me inferior. I asked God why he had made me a girl when I would have been able to do so much more for him as a man. The thought that came back to me was: "What you need to do in your life, you can do better as a woman."

Chapter Two

One time while watching the moon and stars as the clouds drifted by, I wondered, *What will happen in my future? Will there be fame in my life? The possibilities are endless!* But then I thought about God. Would I forget Him? Would He leave me?

"Oh God, one thing I ask," I prayed. "Forsake me not, oh Lord, through trials be with me. Should I lose sight of Thee, Lord, turn me back. Forsake not me! Though trials tempt me, lure me on, I love Thee still, Thou Holy One."

I knew my own tendency towards straying from His way.

Being at school was such a delight for me. I learned so much! I even won a drawing contest one time, and my prize was a book, which I still have, and two dollars. I don't remember what I did with those two dollars.

When I was fifteen, my parents made me quit school to help with all the work and the smaller children at home. At the same time, one of my classmates also quit school—but her parents wanted her to finish. Oh how I wished that could have been me! I remember going swimming in my new red swimsuit. There was a dugout, a hollow where the road builder had removed a lot of ground to build a road. It created a waterhole, surrounded on three sides by trees and a lot of underbrush, not far from our house. I loved to go swimming in it with the neighbourhood kids and my brothers and sisters. That was our summer pastime.

One time I was alone at this dugout, as everyone else had gone home. When I got out of the water, some older boys came to the dugout and I remember one of them leering at me as I went into the area in the bush where we changed our clothes. Nobody could see me there. As I took off my wet swimsuit, I remember thinking, *I have to hurry before those guys think of anything stupid to do.*

The next Sunday afternoon, the guy who had been leering at me at the dugout saw me. He was with his girlfriend. I said hi to them, and he looked at me in a very strange and weird way. I didn't remember him doing anything to me at the dugout.

Many years later, I was told that he had died at a young age.

The young people in our community, mostly teenagers, would gather in different homes on Sunday evenings, and one of their favourite places to gather was at our home. Mom and Dad enjoyed the young people and didn't mind having them at our house. Sometimes we would turn on the radio, or someone would bring a guitar and we would play music and dance. My parents thought that dancing was wrong, and I finally decided that I would listen to them. But my thought then was, and it still is, that the dancing we did was much better for us than sitting in the back seats of cars and drinking beer or other alcohol. You know what that could lead to!

We had almost no outside influences in our community. Nobody I knew had a TV. I didn't know anything about illegal drugs or about homosexuality or "free love." The radio was our only connection to the outside world; my friend and I used to sneak into her brother's room when he wasn't home to listen to a radio show called "Teen Scene."

Summer brought many activities to enjoy. I delighted in watching thunderstorms, listening to the thunder, and seeing the great streaks of lightning flash across the sky! I wanted to watch everything that was going on in the sky. This prompted me to write the following:

Thunder makes me feel so much closer to God. He seems so close and so real then. My heart aches because it was so full of Him. In silence I seem to drift away from Him with earthly cares. Thunder is loud, declaring Him who rules all. He is King, there is none who is more awesome than He! Can you not hear it? Feel it? He is here, among us, showing us His power. Our Jesus who died so we can live with Him in Glory forever!

My family then moved to a homestead several miles away from our community, and we moved a large workshop there that my dad had built. This became our first temporary home on that land.

There were many bears in that area, so we had to be careful not to leave any food outside. At times wolves could be heard howling into the night through the thin walls. It was such an eerie, lonesome sound that it made me shiver inside.

By now I felt I was quite grown up and I had God in my life.

My former, and favourite, teacher ran a sewing circle where we learned to do needlework and memorize Bible verses. One evening, she took us all for a walk and we sang the song "How Great Thou Art." I remember how great it felt that lovely evening to sing those words while the stars were so bright and beautiful.

She even took me to some church services where I learned more about God. I had hope for the future.

That teacher also gave me a New Testament, and in Grade Five I received a Gideon's Bible. I read those daily. I also promised God that I would read His Word every day. That has made a huge difference in my life! Sometimes, when I didn't have my Bible with me, I'd repeat the verses I had memorized.

Chapter Three

I remember coming to consciousness that day at the swimming dugout. While putting on my dry clothes, I was thinking that they would now cover a totally different person. I ran home as fast as I could, thinking, *I made it!* Then I looked down at my legs and wondered how I had gotten those scratches.

Oh well, I thought. *It doesn't matter. Nothing happened.*

I didn't feel anything. I was just very relieved that those guys were gone when I came out of the bushes that day at the dugout.

On a day shortly after that, I could hardly walk. My hip hurt terribly, so I waited outside until the pain subsided while the rest of my family and some friends went inside. A dear friend stayed with me and I said something to her about her having a happy life but that mine would not be happy until much later. How or why I said that, I don't know.

Once, when I went outside, I heard a noise that caused me to run back inside. I was white as a sheet and scared out of my mind! But it was only the boys herding cows back to the barn.

At seventeen, I had what was called a nervous breakdown. My parents took me to a doctor who prescribed antidepressants that made me sleep most of the time. That was no good. My mother needed me to help her, so she burned those pills.

I still believed in God and read my Bible every day. I also felt that I should be baptized and wanted to do that in an evangelical church where I knew that they believed as I did. But that church split and then my parents convinced me to be baptized in their church. After I was baptized, I wished that I could die right then, because I knew that there was no way I could live the rest of my life without sinning. However, I was determined to live my life as true to God as I possibly could!

That summer, my cousin asked my parents if one of us could ride with her to another province to visit her parents. They allowed me to go with her. It was a most delightful time for me. We spent lots of time singing with my cousins at the piano, visiting other cousins in the area where my parents had grown up up, and listening to my uncle pray and read the Bible in the mornings. That impressed me so much that I wished my dad would do it with us!

I will always remember that trip. I'm so thankful for what that cousin did for me. She has a very special place in my heart.

At eighteen, I had a cancer scare when I discovered a lump in my left breast. Thank God, the cyst was benign. The doctor then told me that although these cysts would continue to grow, they would probably disappear if I were to have children.

My dream of becoming a nurse was still with me, so I talked to our religious leader about it. He said that it would be okay if I served our community as a nurse, but that I would serve God better if I got married and had children.

Now I had received two messages telling me to marry and have children, and no messages telling me to become a nurse. And where would I go to finish school and get the necessary training?

My first job was babysitting three beautiful children. They were so cute! One day I wasn't feeling well and the youngest came and sat with me for a long time. For her to do that was such a comfort to me. They lived in town near my cousin, so I was able to stay with her during the week.

At a loss as to what to do with my life, since I couldn't finish school, I began to host special social gatherings at our house. I invited the neighbourhood young people to our house and we had a lot of fun. There was one guy who came who I thought was especially handsome!

My oldest sister's wedding brought me some interesting insights. In the evening, I found an empty cherry whiskey bottle. I filled it with water and passed it around to those who were outside. It was so much fun to watch the guys think that they were getting drunk from it! They didn't even notice that it was only water.

Another incident I will always be thankful for is what happened after the wedding. Everyone left our place and went to a dance outside. We were having a lot of fun dancing when a guy picked me up and started to carry me to his car! I fought him, and guess what? That handsome guy from our neighbourhood came to rescue me! He knew what kind of a scoundrel was picking me up, so he just tapped him on the shoulder and said, "Don't you do that!" That scoundrel let go of me right away! That really gave me some major respect in my heart for that handsome guy! He also made sure I got home safely that night.

Our relationship grew after that incident and it wasn't long before he asked me out on a date. He was often the one to pick me up from my cousin's place and take me home to my family.

I sometimes wondered why he didn't come to see me during the week. Most other couples, when they became quite serious about each other, did that. But he didn't seem to want to be with me as much as I wished he would.

When he came to see me one time, my dad gave him a beer. He was so pleased by that! What I didn't know was that this guy really enjoyed alcohol.

Chapter Four

Over the years I had a lot of nightmares. The first one was too gruesome to share. It was so real that it haunted me for a long time.

Another dream kept recurring; I was always running from someone who was trying to hurt me, always trying to get away, sometimes from the bush into a house, or sometimes through a window into a house. Sometimes it was one or more bears chasing me. I remember waking up just as one of the bears in my dream managed to get his nose into the door. My heart beat so fast that when it started to slow down, I was scared it would stop.

One time the dream was too visual. I saw someone being stabbed and left to die. The horror of witnessing someone being killed was very vivid.

The nightmares got so bad that I implored God to take them away. Often I went to sleep praying that I wouldn't dream anything.

My last dream like this involved me running from the woods into a house, into one room after another. Finally I found myself in a room in the middle of the house. There were no windows. The killer, or at least I thought it was a killer, came right into the room. I was under the bed and he stopped in front of me and said, "I won't hurt you." I took this dream to mean that I had been running from myself.

After a while, most of the dreams stopped.

I had some reservations about getting married, but I prayed about it and eventually felt that it was okay for me to marry that handsome guy from our neighbourhood. We had a church wedding. After a regular sermon, we had to stand up in front of the church and say our vows. We then had a meal at my parents' home. I'd made a pink brocade dress for the evening.

Later, on our way to our new life, we got a flat tire!

So at nineteen, I became his wife. I had high hopes that we would have a long and happy marriage, but I was naive and totally unprepared for this stage in my life. Our first home was a one-room suite in the same town where I was still babysitting those three cute children. My husband had not yet found a job.

I remember walking home alone in the evening one day when a pack of dogs ran up to me. I was scared but didn't let it show. My first instinct was to pat the first dog that came up to me on the head. He let me do that and then they all ran off!

My husband was the third child of a very young mother. Several times when he was a baby, he had nearly died. Twice she had put him down thinking he was gone. She told him many times that she wished he had been able to die then. She'd thought it would have been better to die as a baby and be spared all the hardships of life. But because of this, he grew up thinking he didn't deserve to live. He had a wall around his heart so no one could get inside.

Many years later, I began to see that he was a scared, lonely, sad little boy inside, crying out silently to be wanted but being totally unable to open up that wall. This made him unable to be the husband I needed.

Two years into our marriage, I thought that I had made a big mistake. I didn't feel that my husband really loved me, but I thought that I could make our marriage work as long as I did everything I could to be a good wife.

I was now a mother to our firstborn, a son. Becoming a mother changed me. I had been such a fearful person before he came along, but now I became a mama bear. If anyone tried to hurt my baby, they would have to contend with me!

Chapter Five

Those first years were pretty good. My husband's job took us to a distant and again isolated farm during the summers. There were several other men with their families also working on that farm. We knew most of them. We were a nice little community.

The house we lived in was old, but I made it as comfortable as I could. After our second child was born, I made a bed for her by placing two chairs against the wall with the backs to the room. That way she couldn't roll off and fall to the floor.

I was so proud to have a daughter as well as a son! They came only a year and three months apart.

Our boy had a crib to sleep in. Often he would hold his glass bottle in his hand and drop it to the floor. I think he was trying to figure out in his little mind why it broke apart and made such a funny noise when it hit the floor!

My husband worked on the land harvesting and doing many other chores. One of his chores was to take water up the side of the hill so we could have running water during the summer. As he drove the water truck high up on the hillside, I watched with some of the women, as well as our children. To my horror, the truck flipped over on its side because the hill was too steep!

There was a moment when I thought he might be dead, but then he climbed out of the passenger side window. What a relief that was!

Another time, he sent me to pick him up from a field farther away. I didn't have a driver's license and very little experience. I didn't know that the parking brake was on, so I drove a few miles with it on. I was so scared to tell him about it, but he told me, "You didn't do it on purpose!"

Once while we lived there, we had company and my husband kicked me in a way that was only meant to be in fun to him, but it really insulted me. I made such a fuss that he never did it again!

That was the only physical abuse I ever received from him, but he knew how to use barbed words that really hurt. A woman who had experienced both physical and verbal abuse once said to me, "Abusive words are like razor cuts under the skin. They hurt, but no one can see them." She also said, "Bruises heal, but words hurt a lot longer."

When the farm work was done, we moved to a small town where my husband got a really good job. We left most of our friends and family back home. That was tough, but the best thing was that one of my siblings and his family already lived in our new town. Even with that, though, it took more than two years before I finally began to think of that town as my home.

A lovely Indigenous woman became my friend and helped me feel more at home there. She'd borrow a cup of sugar or flour, and then the next day she'd bring me a pie! That was better than getting the sugar or flour back. Mom had taught me to always return a little more than I had borrowed, but this was even better.

We visited often, and many times her husband and mine went hunting for moose together.

One time her son and mine were having an argument and I heard her son call my son an Indian. She and I got a good laugh out of that one!

We lived in a small mobile home that had plenty of storage but very little room. Sometimes bigger people came to visit us, but our little bathroom was almost too small for them to get into.

My youngest child, a tiny, beautiful girl, was born during that time. I decorated a cardboard box with my pink brocade dress and placed it on the portable washing machine. That's where she slept, because there was no room for a third crib in the mobile home.

We made friends with some of the people from our home community who lived in this new town. One time, a family we knew came to visit. The parents were very abusive to their children and I couldn't stand it. I prayed about it after they left and I decided to write a letter to the mother about her responsibility to show Christ's love to her children. It felt as though Jesus was with me right there while I wrote the letter.

I then showed the letter to my husband (I didn't know at the time that he couldn't read or write) and he said I shouldn't give the letter to the woman, and so I faced a dilemma—should I obey my husband or should I do what I believed Jesus wanted me to do? My upbringing really emphasized obedience to the husband. I wavered and kept thinking that I should bring the letter to that mother anyway.

A month went by, and then the mother died. I felt that I had failed both her and God. I couldn't forgive myself for that.

Being so far away from most of my old friends and family was hard. I spent most of the time alone with my children.

Work and my husband's new friends kept him away a lot, and the men he worked with always had alcohol handy. They saw that he enjoyed it and supplied him with it a lot of it. That kept him away from us many evenings. Too often he came home drunk.

This is about the time when depression began to really take a hold on me.

In the Bible, I read about ways to make myself happier. I began to focus on things that are beautiful, since I already enjoy visual things. One helped me a lot: *"Finally, my brothers and sisters, whatever is true, whatever is noble, whatever is right, whatever is pure, whatever is lovely, whatever is admirable—if anything is excellent or praiseworthy—think about such things"* (Philippians 4:8).

Looking closely at nature and watching the sky can be fascinating. There is always something interesting in it—clouds, sunrises and sunsets, stars, and the moon. And I enjoy colour in everything, even snow in bright sunlight. Have a good look sometime! You'll see fields of diamonds in the snow.

My sister-in-law got me into painting at her friend's house, which I enjoyed very much. This is when I learned to use oil paints. I also began to take courses in the visual arts. I even won a scholarship in that course! It was a great way to express myself.

A particular verse from the Bible stood out to me one day as I was reading it. I didn't know why at that time, but now it makes sense:

If thou hast run with the footmen, and they have wearied thee, then how canst thou contend with horses? and if in the land of peace, wherein thou trustedst, they wearied thee, then how wilt thou do in the swelling of Jordan? (Jeremiah 12:5, KJV)

Chapter Six

God gave me a dream when things were very hard, and it sums up what was happening in my life. In the dream, I was trying to walk up a mountainside on very rocky ground while carrying an old woman who kept falling apart. I could hardly keep her together. I was also carrying a man who was lying on my back. Was God trying to tell me something?

I've heard other people talk about "affairs of the heart." This is what I began to do. I fantasized about other men, dreaming about how they would love me. I've included this in my story because I want to be real, to show myself as the imperfect woman I am.

A darkness was also coming over me.

I'm no good to God, I thought to myself. *There is so much I should have done differently, so much I've done wrong.*

These thoughts kept running through my mind. The culture in my new town was so different, and I didn't think the people understood me. I thought they might laugh at the peculiar traditions I had been brought up in and not want me around. These fears kept me from making friends with the wives of my husband's co-workers.

Since reading had taken away my pain when I had appendicitis, it became a way for me to block out emotional pain. It didn't help that I felt neglected and saw more and more alcohol in our lives. At home, my reading became obsessive. I escaped reality through books. I neglected my home and my children. Sometimes I think my children turned out well in spite of me, not because of me!

A neighbour, knowing about my interest in reading, once brought me a box full of books. I got really involved in those books and found many fascinating stories. Some were even about demonic powers and oppression. Yikes, so many scary stories!

One writer claimed that the concept of reincarnation fit in with Christianity. I was almost convinced that reincarnation was real when this author claimed that John the Baptist was the reincarnation of Elijah.

During this time, a very strange thing happened one evening after supper. My husband had just gone out to drink with his buddies again and the children were fighting and crying. As I turned to do the dishes, my eyes fell on a knife lying on the kitchen cupboards. The sight of it gave me a very weird, icy feeling. Then I heard a voice say to me, "Why not end this misery? You aren't happy. Your children are miserable. You can all be happy in your next lives. You can end all this right now!" The words came from somewhere outside of me. They were as clear as if someone was speaking right into my ear.

My eyes fell on the knife. Then I felt a very strong power trying to wrench control from me.

Suddenly, the truth of this horrible suggestion hit me! This was not coming from God. This was evil itself. Murder and suicide! I prayed, *God help me!*

With all the strength I had, I picked up the knife and washed it. Then I quickly put it out of my sight into the kitchen drawer. My knees went weak and I had to sit down.

With tears streaming down my cheeks, I hugged my children. "Why are you crying, Mommy?" they asked. They didn't know what had just happened.

The Bible was, and still is, a constant in my life. Every day I found much comfort in the psalms. So many verses conveyed the message that I should just trust God. So I hung on.

One day while reading a magazine, I saw that someone had written in and asked about reincarnation. The writer of the magazine quoted this verse from Hebrews 9:27: *"Just as people are destined to die once, and after that to face judgment..."* The King James Version says, *"And as it is appointed unto men once to die, but after this the judgement..."*

Understanding and peace flooded my heart. That was my answer. The truth hadn't been in that other book. The Bible holds the truth, the whole truth. Suddenly, joy from deep inside of me started bubbling up! What a relief that was! I didn't have to wonder about that anymore.

I was alone with my children most of the time. I often opened the Bible and found something from God to help me. One day this verse got my attention:

"For your Maker is your husband—the Lord Almighty is his name—the Holy One of Israel is your Redeemer; he is called the God of all the earth. The Lord will call you back as if you were a wife deserted and distressed in spirit—a wife who married young, only to be rejected," says your God. "For a brief moment I abandoned you, but with deep compassion I will bring you back. In a surge of anger I hid my face from

you for a moment, but with everlasting kindness I will have compassion on you," says the Lord your Redeemer. (Isaiah 54:5–8)

These verses meant so much to me!

Many Sunday mornings I woke up with the thought, *"Go to church."* There were several churches in this town, so I went to one, but it only held services once a month. Unsure of where to go next, it took me a while to then find a Full Gospel Church.

There were days when I felt too raw inside to go, but the insistence that I go to church was so strong that I went anyway. Other times I felt that I just couldn't do it, but then someone would give me a smile, a handshake, or a hug and I knew I would be back.

One time a little girl, in her mother's arms, reached out and hugged me. I felt like I had just gotten a hug from Jesus!

I am so thankful that God insisted that I go to church. My children were brought up in that church and all were baptized by its pastor.

Chapter Seven

I was once given a dream, a beautiful dream—I was in a waiting room. The door in front of me was closed, but the love that seeped through from around the door was so awesome that I knew nothing could be better. I knew that love was worth dying for—and it's worth living for, too! It is better than anything on earth.

When I woke up, I felt like that love was wrapped around me. The memory of that dream is still so vivid that I will never forget it. God's love for me and you is beyond anything in this world!

By the time our youngest child went to school, I also went back to school. I learned to type there. I even got to dissect a bullfrog and make a drawing of everything I saw inside it. That was interesting! After two years in upgrading my education, I received my grade twelve diploma.

My husband had a good job, and financially we were all right. We always had enough food and clothing. He liked to shop for groceries. Anything on sale was brought home, even if we already had lots of it. I don't know how many boxes of crackers we had at one time, but it was a lot!

One time while we were eating supper, the TV was on. Since it was in view of the kitchen, I saw a dramatization of rape. It upset me and I couldn't eat very much after seeing and hearing that. It was a documentary about rape on university campuses and my husband and my daughter wanted to watch it. My son and I stayed in the kitchen and tried to drown it out.

I went downstairs after trying to concentrate on cleaning the kitchen and did some mending.

When I was finished my upgrading, I got a job as a receptionist. My husband said I wouldn't last a month. After two years there, I knew that it wasn't the right fit for me, so I gave up that job and went to work at a college in our town. There, I took a course and did a practicum in tutoring adults in basic literacy. Part of my reason for going into that field was because I saw how hard it was for my husband to function in his job without reading or writing. That was a much better fit for me.

I thoroughly enjoyed working with adults teaching literacy. I had some of the most delightful students! Some of them were so eager to learn that I could hardly keep up with them. One student had no formal education at all, but she figured out algebra on her own!

On a Friday, after an Al-Anon meeting, a friend told me that her daughter had been the victim of incest by her son. She needed to talk, so I gave her a ride home. I told her that I had once been approached that way by my oldest brother when I was about eight years old. I pushed him away and ran to play with the other kids. Many days later, when I was playing with my two youngest brothers, I didn't touch their privates but I picked each one up and held them against me inappropriately. I felt immediately very ashamed of it and never did it again.

As my friend and I spoke, I began to shake uncontrollably. I couldn't remember any terror from that experience at all with my oldest brother, so I didn't understand why I was shaking so hard.

On the way home from her place, something huge, dark, shapeless, ugly, and very frightening tried to break through to my conscious mind. I started to cry.

Why did you do this to me? I thought. *No, I can't remember this!* I shut it out of my mind. I was okay by the time I got home.

I couldn't stop thinking about what had happened with my friend's children, and my reaction to it puzzled me even more. Had something happened to me? What was it? Could I really have blocked out of my mind something too horrible to remember? Did this have anything to do with what had happened at that swimming hole when I was sixteen?

During this time, a terrible temptation came my way. The devil is not a gentleman and he threw a major hurdle at me. My husband sometimes brought some of his buddies home for meals, and one time he even asked one of them to stay with us for a while. That man once made a pass at me while my husband was outside. I stopped him, but my husband became obsessed about that. He told me that if I had an affair, then he could too!

One morning, I woke up and it seemed to me that time stood still. I could choose what I wanted. I could have this guy if I wanted him badly enough. If my husband was dead, I would be free.

The thought came to me, *That could be arranged.*

But I couldn't wish my husband to die in any way because of me.

Immediately, time resumed. I had made my choice.

The next guy my husband brought home was more insistent. He did everything he could to seduce me. My husband saw this and realized that I was flattered by the man's attention, and he didn't stop it. Instead my husband set me up many times so that I had to take his drinking buddy home. It was only by God's grace that I was able to stop myself from running away with him!

I lived in a fog during that time. I cannot believe that I allowed many wrong things to happen, but I couldn't give myself to him.

It was during this time that I felt a very real desire to split myself in two, meaning that I would split my mind so that I could do what I was so tempted to do yet also be the woman I knew God wanted me to be. I think this is a type of mental illness—multiple personalities. But I knew that whatever either personality did, the person in this body would still be the one responsible to God. I couldn't give in to that! Then that temptation left me.

When I finally came out of that fog, I went to my Heavenly Father and told Him everything. His wonderful and awesome love is unbelievable. He showed me a visual picture of me in His arms as I cried. He comforted me in a way that I will never forget.

Still, I kept replaying in my mind the images of that man who had tried to seduce me. Finally I framed each image in my mind and brought it to Jesus. In my mind, I could see Him carrying each one away. That stopped my obsessions about that man!

I went to work after that Al-Anon meeting on Monday feeling a little unbalanced. By noon I was shaking so bad that I couldn't think straight. I thought I might throw up or mess myself. I cried, thinking that I would go out of my mind.

My co-worker didn't know what to do. She was at a complete loss as to how to deal with me. I remember wishing she would call somebody who would know what to do.

I went to my supervisor, who saw that I was in a crisis. She called a counsellor for me. After the counsellor had talked with me and made an appointment for me to see him that afternoon, my supervisor stayed with me. I told her that for many years I had felt like I had a snake inside me and had ignored it, but now it had to come out. I didn't know what poison it would inflict on me. I also felt that I needed someone who could bring me back if I went out of my mind. I didn't know what I would do.

She sat with me for over an hour. By then I had calmed down and was able to continue my work until I could speak with the counsellor.

After work, as I spoke with the counsellor, I felt better. My stomach was just a little queasy. I knew I needed to remember something that had happened to me, so I tried, but I couldn't even pinpoint when or where it had happened. There was nothing in my memory of any incident that could have triggered such a violent reaction from me.

The counsellor suggested that I write down anything that would help me to remember.

When I got home, I tried word associations and just let words flow from my pen. I didn't even need to read what I wrote down.

After several agonizing days and nights of trying to remember, and of being afraid that I would remember, I managed to write down most of my feelings. By then I knew this reaction had to have something to do with what had happened at that waterhole dugout when I was sixteen, but all that came to mind was a fast, hazy, underwater swim. I didn't want to be alone or be at home with my husband. I thought he wouldn't understand, and that I might black out or scream uncontrollably. I didn't know what I would do. I didn't trust myself.

I found that writing what I was feeling was a great way to express what I couldn't talk about. I wrote letters to God in which I expressed the things I was feeling. Every time I felt anything intensely, I wrote it down. I wrote lots of poems and little stories.

Almost every summer, we went camping with my oldest brother and his family. At first we had a tent trailer, and later we bought a small trailer. One time we arrived at our campsite late in the evening, cooked supper, and went to bed. In the morning, a big black bear was in our campsite. My husband told that bear, in a firm but calm voice, "Get away from us! Go away!"

To my surprise, the bear got up and walked away!

Another time, my sister-in-law and I hiked to the top of a mountain. Part of the trip was on a skytram, but the last mile we went on foot. What an awesome sight it was to see the town so far below us. Other mountaintops were visible all around us! My heart was filled with the majesty of our great Creator God! I remember standing on top of that mountain singing "How Great Thou Art."

When I was forty-one years old, my lovely oldest daughter got married to a wonderful, handsome man. I was so proud of them both. They had a beautiful wedding! Her dad walked her up the aisle as proud as could be. I was so happy for her.

My daughter has since given me two grandsons! When the first one was born, I got a ride to visit her in a friend's airplane. When the second one was born, we went by car.

The love one has for their grandchild is so incredible. It has been hard to be so far away from them. I wished I could stay with them. I couldn't be more proud to be their grandma!

Chapter Eight

One day we were invited to go to tea at our neighbour's house, and my husband decided to go on ahead of me. I was home alone, still feeling some of the fear I'd had felt earlier. Just after he left, I quite clearly heard the sound of twigs breaking all around me. It was coming from the walls! But I wouldn't let fear overtake me.

Then the sounds stopped and I forced myself to walk out of the house and go for tea. By the time I got there, I was okay again.

The more I tried to follow what I believed was right, the more I was judged by my husband and my oldest brother on what I didn't do right. I felt like I was walking a tightrope with no room for even the smallest error. But I am human, and it is an impossible task.

One evening, after everyone was in bed, I walked into our bedroom and felt in my spirit that there were three or four spiritual beings doing something by my husband's head. One of those beings seemed to be female and she began to come towards me! Immediately I got down on my knees and began to pray. They must have left, because I couldn't sense those spirits after that.

Another time as I entered our bedroom one night, I felt an intense hatred towards my husband as he lay passed out on the bed. I knew it was wrong to feel that way, so I got down on my knees and asked God to forgive me. He gave me a heart full of pity for my husband. My husband had so much going against him; no wonder he needed something to numb his pain.

One time while I was working, I had to go to an education conference in a major city. The room I was given was just below the top floor and I was told there had once been a nightclub on the top floor. My room had the biggest bed I had ever seen in my life. I thought it was odd to have such a bed, which was the size of three twin beds put together in a room for a single person!

On the ceiling of that room was a rust-brown area. It looked like something had seeped through from the room above. My thoughts, always busy, tried to figure out why it would be there. I imagined that maybe it was blood that paint could not cover. *What unsolved mystery lies behind this?* I wondered. Of course, it could simply have been water and rust stains from pipes overhead.

That night in that big bed, I dreamed that I was struggling violently to free myself from an unwanted demonic hold on my body by someone, or something, to no avail. Still in my dream, I called out, "Jesus! Jesus, help me!" The hold on me released immediately and then I woke up.

My friend, who lives in that city, came to visit me and I asked her to pray with me concerning the dream and the creepy feelings I'd had in that room.

The last night I was there, before I fell asleep, an insistent thought kept intruding into my mind of something flying onto the balcony railing. It seemed to be black, shaped like a raven, and as big as a six-foot-tall man. The sound of the being's landing on the railing wanted to intrude into my hearing. Was it just my imagination, or was I losing my mind? Whatever it was, it was really weird. Through prayer, and through repeating a Bible verse continuously, those impressions left and I was able to sleep.

In church one morning, the assistant pastor asked if anyone needed prayer for healing. Of course I went forward, as did my daughter for her miserable cold. My son also went forward for direction for his future.

It was wonderful to hear the pastor pray for my children. They are so precious to me. I wished my other daughter had been there, too.

When it was time for them to pray for me, I asked for spiritual healing, but I couldn't tell the pastor why I needed it. The pastor prayed concerning Life, battling against the destruction that was at work on me and had been working against me for many years. He prayed for healing for what I didn't know, and that forgiveness would be in me. But I had told him nothing about my life.

I realized I could no longer ignore or fight against God. He loves me. Why would He work towards healing for me if He did not? How did God put those words in the pastor's mouth? It is God's Holy Spirit at work. There is no other explanation.

Early one morning, I woke up with the strong impression that I had to forgive my mother-in-law. I remembered her often telling my husband that she had laid him down several times as a child thinking he was gone—and she wished he could have died then. She had thought it would be better to die as a baby than to live through all the hardships of life.

There were other things I needed to forgive as well in my mind.

It felt good to forgive her for most of it, but I still couldn't feel forgiveness for what her words had done to my husband. For this I said to God, *I am willing myself to forgive her, but right now I cannot feel the forgiveness.* This went on for about an hour.

Then we got the phone call that my mother-in-law had died. I am so grateful that God gave me that time to forgive her before she was gone. I don't know if that helped her or not, but it certainly helped me deal with her death.

After years and years of hearing what a bad person I was, I was beginning to believe it. I felt like I didn't deserve to live. I felt totally trapped. Divorce was wrong. I'd been taught that all my life and I believed it. I just wanted to die. Hearing songs about heaven made me want to be there so desperately that I couldn't stop crying when I heard them.

I often had thoughts about how I could die, but I wasn't able to figure out what to tell my children. If I told them that they still had God, how could they trust Him if He hadn't been enough for me? Then I began to see that God did not want me dead. My life was more precious to Him than even my marriage.

I went to see the counsellor again to ask more questions. Did this have anything to do what had happened at that swimming hole when I was sixteen?

"Will the feelings come slowly, maybe, so I can deal with them before I remember all of it?" I asked. "Is it really possible that I could have blocked out something for twenty-seven years?"

It all seemed a little unreal to me.

Chapter Nine

One time, as I lay my head on my pillow, I had a vision of someone cutting off my head, complete with bone-crushing severance. I was overwhelmed with an urgent external pressure that I had to immediately kill myself.

I phoned my counsellor just so this thing wouldn't overpower me. I couldn't tell him what I felt, though, because I couldn't describe it. I asked him what I should do and he told me that I could get my husband to bring me to his office; he would be free at eleven o'clock.

I wondered if I should see a doctor because the pain in my head was so severe. I was shaking uncontrollably and I felt like my skin was crawling. The counsellor kept me on the phone until I felt a little bit in control of myself.

I then phoned my husband, but he didn't answer. I left a message for him to come home right away. When he came home, however, he didn't know what to do with me. That morning, he had asked about where all our income tax forms were. While I waited for him, I got them ready. In fact, I felt like I had to give him everything right away because I might not be around later. He said he needed to go to the bank anyway, to buy retirement savings bonds.

"Is this is how you'll deal with what's happening with me, just ignore it?" I asked. "That bank can wait. We can go see the counsellor or you can take me to a doctor."

We went to town and he dropped me off at the hospital, where one of the nurses advised me to go to the emergency room.

The doctor on-call at the ER talked with me for a long time. He'd seen an article in a newspaper about sexual abuse and read much of it to me. He asked me if I believed in God, and I told him that I was a Christian but that I felt deserted, even by God. He said that God must have allowed this to happen to me for some reason—maybe so that I would be able to protect my daughters from a similar situation. He suggested that I needed to pray and ask God to take this burden from me. He also made an appointment for me to see a psychologist the next day.

I then asked for a shot to relax me, which I got. The doctor also gave me a bottle of homeopathic medicine instead of prescribing tranquilizers.

It was noon when my husband and I left the hospital. I tried to rest when I got home. I could lie down, but I couldn't sleep. In the evening, my headache had subsided but I still felt agitated. Since I still couldn't sleep, I decided I had to go for a walk. My husband went with me out in a storm. We walked for about forty-five minutes. We were very cold, but I felt much better.

That night, I woke up every few hours—but I did sleep.

The following day I went back to work. I felt a little abnormal, but I needed to do normal things. I was much better by that evening. I decided not to use the herbal medicine I had gotten until I felt desperate again.

Coming home from work one day, my daughter looked at me in a way I couldn't ignore. I asked her what was wrong and she said, "Dad told me that you molest little boys!"

I was shocked! Then I had to tell her about what had happened with my brothers when I was about eight years old—that I had been approached by my oldest brother sexually and that I had done something inappropriate with my then youngest brothers.

I understood then that my husband had said this so that my daughters would keep my grandsons away from me. That was hard to hear, even harder than hearing him phone my siblings and tell them what an awful woman I was.

At work, part of my ongoing training in teaching adults involved taking a drama course. One day the instructor called me and wanted to meet with me. The first thing he said was, "How are you?" I couldn't hold inside what was going on in my mind. The tears just flowed. He was very understanding and made me promise that I would call him before I did anything to myself.

Much later, when I went back to thank him for his part in saving my life, he really didn't think he had done much, but God had used him to get me to talk.

Many questions kept going through my head. Had I been angry at men for making me feel that I was inferior to them? Did I blame my husband for all my pain? Had I really been terribly unfair to him? He has done many good things. We had never gone hungry. We had always had a home. He'd also helped a lot with the cooking, but not the messes. My cooking, too, often wasn't good enough, so then he would take over. That often caused me to just go to bed. It was hard to feel useless in my own kitchen.

When I had gallbladder surgery, my husband sat by my bed for a long time. My fears were still with me, however, and the painkillers seemed to produce weird hallucinations; I was being held tightly from behind, like I was being sexually assaulted. Then I felt like I was floating on the ceiling. There seemed to be many people all around me. I was thirsty and telling my husband, "I haven't had my coffee yet!"

When the hallucinations ended, I was back in bed again and he and I were the only ones in the room. After that experience, I asked the nurses to stop giving me those painkillers.

Chapter Ten

Al-Anon, a support group for those living with alcoholics, was helpful to me. Their twelve-step program and weekly meetings helped me to call on and receive God's help in the crazy world of alcohol. I went regularly and also joined a survivor's support group.

One of the things I was encouraged to do was make a list of things I would still like to do, things I wanted to see more of in the world. I began to think about where I would like to go. At that time I didn't know where to travel, but thinking about it helped me plan for the future.

An appointment had been made for me with a psychologist because of my desperation earlier, so I went to see him. I felt a little uneasy knowing that he was very busy and had made time for me on the insistence of the ER doctor. I told him that I felt much better. I also told him what had been going on without going into much detail. He made me see that what I was going through would take time to work out, even if he could see me every day. He was very busy and could only see me once every two weeks for a while, and then maybe once a week when his schedule opened up. I just wished there was a Christian woman psychologist I could go see.

The next day, our employer gave us a day for professional development. One co-worker came to me and said, "I want to talk with you. I've been dreaming about you."

After lunch, that co-workers and I went into the library and she said that in her dream she had seen my face and I had looked incredibly sad.

"What's happening with you?" she asked.

I told her a little bit about what I'd been going through, that I felt totally deserted. She told me that she had read somewhere that when God seems the furthest away, He's really carrying you.

On one of my handouts from that day's workshops, I wrote, "God is closer when He seems far away. In times of greatest need, He carries you." I wanted to be able to concentrate on that when I felt desperate again.

That afternoon, I began to feel claustrophobic. I was sitting too far away from the door and there were many people in the room. Chairs had been stacked up and they were in the way. By 4:00 p.m., I just had to get out of there. I even took some of the medicine the doctor had given me.

I went to my counsellor to see if I could talk with him and also return a book on anger that I had borrowed. He was busy with another client. I spoke with the receptionist, but I don't think I made much sense to her. I asked her if the counsellor accepted phone calls during the weekend or in the evenings and she said he probably would. I felt better later, so I did not call.

That evening, my family had a birthday party for my son. I managed to bake a cake and relax. Sleep came after my daughter and her husband left.

One Friday, my husband tried to tell me that I shouldn't worry about what had happened in the past. There was no use in getting ulcers over it.

I told him, "I may have gotten sexually assaulted in my mouth!"

This is when he told me about what had happened to him. "When I was about seven or eight, the neighbour's boy grabbed me and tried to do that to me. He pinned my arms down and sat on my chest. I wouldn't open my mouth. There was no way I would open my mouth. How I wish I would have bitten him so hard that he'd never want to do that again. That boy was two years older than I was."

We talked a lot, and sometimes it felt as if there was no solution to our problems. Would we survive as a couple? I didn't want to sleep with him. He hadn't really been interested in me that way before I began this journey, but now he was hurt that I had trouble with it.

I knew I couldn't stay with him if the drinking continued, but I couldn't make a decision right then. He wanted me to tell him if I wanted to stay or not. He told me that if I went to a different church, he might come with me.

On Monday, I photocopied a few papers for my sister and left one paper right-side-up on the photocopier. The paper had information about our survivor's support group, and the only man who works in our building saw it and wanted to know about the group. I told him only a little, but I gave him copies to use if he wished and told him what workbook we used. This made me very uncomfortable.

Being "found out" by someone, together with all the reading I had done on the weekend, made me realize that I had been assaulted at that dugout—but what had actually happened still didn't surface.

I went home that day and told my husband that I wanted to go for a drive. I needed to be alone. He had me check the oil in my car before I left. Once I was in the car, I turned up the music as loud as I could. I felt my heart vibrating with the beat.

Wanting desperately for God to show Himself, I stopped by a lake and prayed for a while. I asked God why he hadn't been at that dugout, why He hadn't stopped the boys from what whatever it was they had done, but I didn't get an answer. I so desperately wanted Him to show Himself. However, I gained the sure knowledge that He loved me.

On the way home, I needed to scream. I didn't know if I *could* scream, since I couldn't remember ever screaming before. It came out hesitantly at first, but then I manged to scream right from the bottom of my being. I had my music on as loud as I could stand it and I screamed most of the way home.

I think I got out some of the screaming I had not been able to do back at the waterhole. That made me feel much better.

How do I explain the hollowness I felt inside? Maybe you've felt it, too. It was an achy, awful feeling that just wouldn't go away.

By that afternoon, I knew that I had to go see my counsellor or take some more of that medicine. Since he'd told me I didn't need the medication, I thought I'd better go see him. He had very little time, but he had said I could come.

When I got there, I told him how I felt. I told him that my mouth hurt, that I had trouble breathing, and that I felt just dreadful inside. It took a lot of effort to speak. I wanted to revert to speaking in my first language, a German dialect, and my words came out funny and disassociated.

After talking about it, I became calmer and was able to breathe better.

Then it was time to go. When he gave me a hug, the tears came. It didn't hurt so much while he held me. He just comforted me and said, "There, there." It felt so good that someone was there for me.

But I wondered how my problems were affecting him. I worried that it might be too much for him, that he might not want to see me anymore.

Chapter Eleven

As time went on, our son and youngest daughter left home. Now there was no buffer between my husband and me. He no longer held anything back, and I became angrier and angrier.

By this time, he was more interested in church, and one Sunday my husband took me to a different church. The preacher there talked about anger, saying, "Anger turned outward, if not dealt with, leads to homicide. And anger turned inward, if not dealt with, leads to suicide."

After the service, I thanked him and told him that I had needed to hear that. He said he had known he had to preach about anger, but he hadn't known who it was for. For this message, I am very grateful.

While I worked at the college where I lived, my co-workers began to encourage me to see if I would be accepted into a Visual Arts program in a big city about a five-hour drive away. One of my sisters already lived there. I didn't have to go, but wouldn't it be nice to know that I could?

I applied. I was accepted. I wanted to go.

I had an appointment to see a psychologist in that city, so we went. From there, I was referred to a psychiatrist and was admitted to the hospital. The doctor put me on an antidepressant and kept me in the hospital for two weeks to make sure that the medicine would work. My husband wanted to buy me a Cadillac at that time! He thought his drinking and treatment of me had been what put me in the hospital.

This is another personal writing I did at the time:

Voices

There are so many voices, who do I listen to? What is really true? "Take care of yourself. Before you can take care of others you must take care of yourself." (Support Group)

You have become so selfish! You weren't like this before you started going to those support groups!" (Husband)

It's guilt talking. He'll never change, they all say that!" (Others at Al-Anon)

"Be strong, you can handle it." (A book I'm reading)

"Those big trucks I see so often on the highway are solid, like a brick wall. No one inside would be hurt if a small car ran into one. Don't even think it! Your pain would only be shifted onto your family." (Me)

There are too many voices. "God where are you? Where were you? Didn't I call on you for help? I can't remember, Why didn't you stop them? Why can't I remember?" (Me)

"If it was really rape, I could understand! You were a virgin, I know that!" (husband)

My mouth hurts. I want to vomit. Please hold my head. It's too heavy for me. I'm only feeling sorry for myself. (Me)

"Are you hearing me, God? In church today they said to give my burdens to you. If only I could physically take them from me and hand them over to you. If I could just see you taking them! If I write this out will it help? How do I make sense of all the voices? Will it help to sit down and think about the things I wish for my abusers, bring me to where I can honestly work out the hurt and the anger: Could I, at this point, wish only good things for them? How co-dependant am I? Can I make it on my own? Should I try?" (Me)

"What hold has he got on you?" (Counsellor)

"As long as there is a spark of hope, work it out!" (Me)

"I have to support you so you can give money to that preacher. (Husband)

"Divorce him. That's what I did with my wife, and I've never been happier." (A co-worker)

"What you do you really want? Tell me! You'd really rather be rid of me, wouldn't you? Isn't that right? What the neighbour's wife does for him, you wouldn't do and I wouldn't ask you to. He's really mean! We could split the money in the bank, and you could have everything you want out of the house." (Husband)

I want to get out of here, to get away from this life! Let me outta here!

These are my burdens, Lord. Please let the true voice overcome the others. Please lift me out of this confusion. Thank you for helping me. (Me)

After I was released from the hospital, my husband and I went to see an instructor at the college. I'm not sure why he took me there, since he had said there was no way I could go to that college. That night, he parked our motor home in the college parking lot. It was almost unbearable to think that I had been accepted to attend that college but wouldn't be able to go!

God is so incredibly gracious. Even though I wanted someone to rescue me so badly that it must have shown, He still made a way for me to begin healing in earnest.

When we got home again, these verses in the Bible really stood out to me:

Be strong and courageous. Do not be afraid or terrified because of them, for the Lord your God goes with you; he will never leave you nor forsake you. (Deuteronomy 31:6)

Depart, depart, go out from there! Touch no unclean thing! Come out from it and be pure, you who carry the articles of the Lord's house. But you will not leave in haste or go in flight; for the Lord will go before you, the God of Israel will be your rear guard. (Isaiah 52:11–12)

Do not be afraid. Stand firm and you will see the deliverance the Lord will bring you today. The Egyptians you see today you will never see again. The Lord will fight for you; you need only to be still. (Exodus 14:13–14)

Chapter Twelve

Dared I go to college in that city? How would I get there? Where would I live? I put out these requests to God, asking Him to show me what I should do. I would go if I could find a female Christian psychologist in the city.

When I went to see my doctor, he gave me a referral to see a psychologist in that city who was the wife of a preacher! She'd only been living there a few months and she worked in the hospital, so my provincial health insurance paid for it.

But where would I live? A dear friend of mine had moved to that city, and I could stay with her.

And how would I get there? I packed what I could in my car. At first I had no bed, just a sponge mattress. But I went.

While living in the city, I had regular appointments with both the psychologist and the psychiatrist. I had my sister nearby, and two special friends. One of these friends I had met while I was in the hospital, and the other friend was the one who owned the house where I stayed.

Through this experience, I began the best healing possible for me.

I'd been dreaming very odd dreams lately. One of them was not overpowering or vivid, but very healing. I was again trying to get away from some bad people. I was with two or three other people. We were all children. I was almost detached, as if I was just watching.

We were trying to hide, so we went into underground passageways that wound in circles and branched off in different directions. We took one way which led us around a corner, but doors were blocking our path. A very big man then opened the doors, and somehow I could see that my head was separated from my body, and yet I was able to speak. My body went through the doors with them, but my head stayed near the steps. The big man asked me if I wanted to come, but I said, "No."

Someone then took my head and body and put them into a pool of water just inside the doors. It was like a huge jacuzzi filled with a special kind of water. It looked like pure water but something special was in it which healed anything. I was put in the water, my head being stuck back on my body, and I saw the band around my neck meld together with the band on my shoulders as I was submerged. This part of the dream was very clear.

I woke up feeling very happy that I was alive, but I didn't remember that unusual dream until a few hours later.

After a year or two in college, I went for therapy at a Christian counselling centre. The counsellor there helped me a lot. He always listened to me and prayed with me. He recommended a book about healing the inner child, and one night after reading it I sat on my bed. In my mind I went through every hurtful memory I could think of, and I cried over them. Then, with each one, I visualized what should have happened, how Jesus would have wanted things to have happened instead of what did happen. That really helped me.

This counsellor also helped me in my struggle with obedience to my husband. There are times when we cannot follow what our husbands want, such as when it is sin. I read about Ananias and Sapphira in Acts 5:1–11. Sapphira was wrong to agree with her husband in lying to the Holy Spirit. It cost her her life!

The counsellor also told me that at one point in the Bible, God told Abraham to listen to his wife. She, who is held up as an example to us of obedience to her husband, also had something for Abraham to listen to: *"But God said to him… "Listen to whatever Sarah tells you…"* (Genesis 21:12)

The counsellor and his wife brought in another spirit-filled Christian who prayed with me to remove any evil spirits that might be affecting me. I knew in my heart that God loved me enough to die for me, because He did, and that God was with me and wanted me to be healed.

I opened my Bible and found a psalm that says:

You have searched me, Lord, and you know me. You know when I sit and when I rise; you perceive my thoughts from afar. You discern my going out and my lying down; you are familiar with all my ways. Before a word is on my tongue you, Lord, know it completely. You hem me in behind and before, and you lay your hand upon me… when I awake, I am still with you. (Psalm 139:1–5, 18)

As I was walking down the street one day, I wondered if I would have enough money to make it through college. As I looked down at the sidewalk, I saw a folded-up twenty-dollar bill lying there! It seemed to me to be a promise from God that I would be all right.

I had received several scholarships, and I had enough money for my tuition. In the summers, I went back home and worked in a women's shelter. Then it was back to the Visual Arts program! By then I was living in a basement suite until I could rent an old house where the rent was low. I worked at the college with my landlady and I received some money from my husband.

In college, I took an English course, but otherwise I focused totally on visual fundamentals, drawing, technical courses in framing and in computer arts, painting, and sculpture.

In my third year, I won the right to create a group of sculptures that are on display in the lawn of the college near one of the entrances. They represent learning and the presence of God in wisdom in our midst.

I even got to travel overseas for two weeks to study art with a group of students from that college. My first few days across the ocean were spent mostly in bed because I got really sick there. I also felt very far away from home. As I read about Paul's shipwreck in the Bible, I was reassured that our group would make it home safely.

As I got better, I decided to take a walk to a museum of art by myself, since the others from my group had gone out earlier. There was a long escalator to the top floor where I saw many beautiful sculptures.

After enjoying so many beautiful works of art that before now I had only read about, I went back down the escalator and felt something invisible jump on my shoulder. It was a weird and very unwelcome feeling.

As I tried to sleep that night, that feeling kept bothering me. I resisted, but it wouldn't go away until I said out loud in my German dialect, "In Jesus's name!" Immediately it left me.

This may seem as strange to you as it did to me, but I believe that a demon was involved. Thank God that the name of Jesus made it go away!

Chapter Thirteen

What are flashbacks, really? Although I've sometimes had momentary, violent visions, I never thought of them as flashbacks. In those visions, I saw people being beaten down, or sometimes even stabbed, but it was always violent. I thought it was just the devil's way of letting me know what he thought of me.

One night, I got a vision of someone grabbing my head and wrenching it forward. It seemed as if I'd had my head turned towards my left. Maybe that was a flashback!

When I thought back to that red swimsuit, I remembered that I never wore it again. Even though I couldn't think of any logical reason why at the time, I ended up giving that lovely swimsuit away.

After a few years in college, my husband decided to move in with me in the city. We wanted to make our marriage work. I had great hopes, but it didn't work out that way. He wanted to control my life in a way that I could not allow. He would only take care of me if I did exactly what he wanted, and before the year was up he moved back to our old town.

It was at this time that I decided I had to divorce him. I needed to be free from all that was still going on with him. I wanted him to face God directly, and it seemed to me that I was in the way.

He did not recognize the divorce and called me often, telling me what an awful woman I was, so I began to record his phone calls. As time went on, I became afraid that my life was in danger on occasions when he came to see my daughter and me.

One Friday, I was told that my husband had been flown to the hospital near me by air ambulance. He was being tested for cancer! I went to visit him and he was very pleased to see me. He held my hand really tightly, like he wanted me to carry his pain. That same night, I did feel intense pain but when I prayed and rejected that pain it went away.

The following Tuesday, the cancer was confirmed. It was so advanced and widespread that they couldn't do anything for him. He was flown back to his hometown.

I didn't want to go back there to see my ex-husband, even though I still cared about his soul, but God had other plans and saw to it that I was with him the week he died. My son flew in from his humanitarian work in another country, and he went to see his dad with my youngest daughter. I drove there alone in my car. I would have dawdled and stayed back longer, but my brother had called me to tell me that a snowstorm was on its way and it would be better if I went right away.

I knew that my children needed me so I went.

When I arrived, my older daughter was already there with her family. It was very good that I went, because we had a kind of reconciliation in the hospital. My ex-husband kept asking my children and me to pray for him. He really wanted to be forgiven for all that he had said about me and to me. He knew his time was up.

I also felt God's presence in a very powerful way. My children and I sat with him throughout the night. While I was resting on a cot, I felt a ball of light coming from God through my ex-husband directly to my heart. Words are so inadequate to describe it, but this event gave me great peace.

Early on Saturday morning, he died. I had sensed that God was at work and nothing on earth could have stopped these things from happening.

My children and my ex-husband's siblings did what they thought was best for his funeral. I was not mentioned in his obituary. My mother was upset about that. At the funeral, the preacher talked about what a great man he had been. It made me feel crazy to hear this until my younger brother, who is also a preacher, said to me that this often happens at funerals because people really want to think the best of a person. I am so thankful that my brother comforted me in this way.

I am so thankful that I am alive. I know that it's not God's doing that these things happen; they happen because people are controlled by sin. The devil desires to control and destroy all of us, but I know that God was with me even when I couldn't feel Him there. He is trustworthy through whatever may come in the future. No one is able to destroy my soul, nor can anyone tear me away from God's love.

After that, I got no more phone calls—no more nasty words meant to hurt me. That chapter of my life was closed. I was not a widow. I was a divorcee, but I was free.

Someone once asked if I now wished that I had stayed with him until he died, but I do not. I was just thankful that I had survived, even though it felt very strange to now be the sole parent of my children.

But God had so much more in store for me.

Chapter Fourteen

Many years ago, I was given this verse by one of my friends: *"I will repay you for the years the locusts have eaten…"* (Joel 2:25). I've just got to tell you what He did for me next!

I asked God for a holiday, a house, and a husband. The first thing that happened was an invitation to visit another country for three weeks. The people there were looking for an artist with my heritage.

I got to make the trip as a journalist with a small group. We met many artists there who took us to visit art galleries, museums, and archaeological digs. There were even a few times when I got to paint with the local artists. Can you think of a better holiday for a person like me? It was an absolutely beautiful time in my life!

That trip happened in March, and in June my youngest daughter and I decided to buy a house together. We were able to move into the house as soon as the paperwork was done. Some of the men from the church we attended at the time helped us move. One of them, a great guy, also tilled the garden for me in our yard.

This home felt so temporary to me that I couldn't help but wonder what was coming next!

My sister kept telling me about a man she knew who had been one her neighbours. This man had a family and his wife had died of cancer. Guess what? It was the same man who had helped my daughter and me move and worked up the garden plot in our yard!

Later, at a church service, I introduced myself to him, and one evening I decided to invite him to come to a charity meal I was volunteering at. I wondered if he might want to come volunteer with me, and even if maybe something could happen between us! He came to that event and enjoyed his time there.

The next thing I knew, he asked me out. Within a couple of months, he asked me if I would marry him! It happened very fast, but since we had both been married before, and we were no longer young, we thought that was all right.

We got married in October that same year. Our wedding was small and we invited our parents, our children, and a few friends. His home became my home.

Now I had all my requests from God: a holiday, a house, and a husband. When God does something, He does it big and He does it best! It's so real and yet sometimes it feels like I'm living in a dream. Life still has its challenges, but it's so much of what I'd prayed for, for so long, that I can't help but praise God! I am so very thankful to God for this new life.

With this marriage, God has given me fully grown step-children. I've also gained more grandsons and granddaughters! God multiplies best. My family is now full and all of the children like each other. So many blessings have been given to me!

The full memory of that sexual assault that happened when I was sixteen remains hidden somewhere deep in my subconscious.

Either I vowed never to remember it, or I believed then that I would die if I remembered it. But the feelings I had shut down have been restored to me, because I have dealt with them. God has made me free. There have been no more nightmares and no more flashbacks. I know now that God never did leave me, that He was with me and hurt with me. I know also that I love Him because He has shown me so many times that He loves me!

Writing my story has been healing for me. Knowing that God loves me is healing. Acknowledging my hurts and praying through them is healing. Letting go of the past as best as I can is healing.

At first when I began working through all the pain, I didn't even want to consider forgiveness. I had to allow myself to feel the anger, pain, betrayal, and injustice of it all. The last thing I needed was to sweep it all under the carpet and pretend it wasn't there. That's what I thought forgiveness was. I have learned that forgiving someone means not getting even or taking revenge against them— but it also means letting go of the anger. It means that we stop letting what happened to control who we are. It means releasing the perpetrators to God.

As I thought about this, I was only willing to think about forgiving the people who had hurt me. To forgive those who had hurt me so much, I had to let go of the anger and the desire to hurt them back.

With God's help, I was able to forgive, but it sometimes seems to be an ongoing process. At times I think I have completely forgiven all the hurts, but then some anger comes back. What I do then is pray about it and make up my mind, again and again, to forgive them.

When I was in grade school, I was given a wall plaque that had written on it the words of Romans 8:28, which says that *all things work together for good to them that love God, to them who are the called according to his purpose*" (KJV). I often thought about that verse and wondered why it was given to me. Some people have told me that it means God allows things to happen to us so that we can later help others who are going through the same things. But I don't believe that God plans for these things to happen to people just so they can help others with the same hurts. My question is, why let it happen at all?

I believe bad things happen because God has given free will to all people. Everyone has a choice to do good or bad. Without free choice, we would be like robots, or like animals at best.

But I also believe that He is able to bring good out of the bad things that happen to us. That means that although we can get hurt by others, God suffers with us through all of it. With that knowledge, we can help others through their hard times. Because of this I have been able to mentor other women going through similar things. It has helped those women who are now my friends.

I know that God is very near to every one of us. Acts 17:27–28 says that *"he is not far from any one of us. 'For in him we live and move and have our being.'"*

I am so glad that I am alive. I would have missed so much—so many blessings, so many good times, so much time with family and good friends who I love! I am so glad that I was given life and that I chose to live it!

God loves everyone, including me and definitely you. Whatever may yet come in life, He will be there with us and for us. I am totally convinced that He is real, that He loves you and me, and that He is very interested and very near to each and every one of us.